57
General A
4630

RESTRICTED

The Information given in this document is not to be communicated, either directly or indirectly, to the Press or to any person not authorized to receive it.

The Pattern 1944 Web Equipment

1946

By Command of the Army Council.

Lic. B B Pred.

THE WAR OFFICE,
    25th June, 1946.

The Naval & Military Press Ltd

Published by

The Naval & Military Press Ltd
Unit 5 Riverside, Brambleside
Bellbrook Industrial Estate
Uckfield, East Sussex
TN22 1QQ England

Tel: +44 (0)1825 749494

www.naval-military-press.com
www.nmarchive.com

In reprinting in facsimile from the original, any imperfections are inevitably reproduced and the quality may fall short of modern type and cartographic standards.

Distribution: Scale "BB" All Arms (Manual of Military Publications).

THE PATTERN 1944 WEB EQUIPMENT

List of Plates.

Plate.
- I. The equipment—unassembled.
- II. The equipment assembled—inside view and waterbottle. (The waterbottle is of aluminium with screw stopper and aluminium cup on the base; the bottle has a capacity of one quart and the cup one pint).
- III. Haversack with shoulder straps.
- IV. Showing operation of quick-release buckle.
- V. Left basic pouch showing double quick-release fastening and alternative method of carrying bayonet.
- VI. Front view.
- VII. Rear view without haversack.
- VIII. Left side showing bayonet on basic pouch, machete in sheath and lightened pick attached to haversack.
- IX. Right side showing rifle slung and position of waterbottle. (The sling is held under shoulder tab and the rifle secured to the belt by a strap, allowing free use of the arm).
- X. Rear view showing method of carriage of the bedding roll under the haversack, and lightened shovel.
- XI. Rear view showing the bedding roll strapped round the haversack, also lightened shovel with a web cover.
- XII. Showing clearance between helmet and shovel blade when in the prone position.
- XIII. Rucksack with closing flap raised to show kit-bag type fastening of main compartment.
- XIV. Rucksack carried with the equipment.
- XV. Man-pack carrier G.S. worn over the equipment.
- XVI. Rucksack attached to the man-pack carrier G.S. worn over the equipment.
- XVII. Equipment assembled for officers.
- XVIII. Front view of the equipment for officers, certain Warrant Officers, N.C.Os. and specialists:
- XIX. Alternative position of articles in front.
- XX. Equipment for those armed with a pistol only.
- XXI. Equipment for non-combatant units.
- XXII. Showing the basic pouch for M.T. drivers.

NOTE.—Plates VIII., X., XI., and XII. show carriage of the respirator haversack. This can be carried in a variety of other positions.

THE PATTERN 1944 WEB EQUIPMENT.

1. Purpose.—The equipment incorporates a new principle of design to enable the load carried to be evenly distributed and well balanced. It was first designed for use in the tropics but has proved equally suitable for all conditions of modern warfare.

The main object has been to reduce the weight of the equipment and to maintain adequate strength in its construction to carry everything needed. This has been achieved by using fine yarn to reduce the thickness of the various types of webbing, and light alloy fittings which have been darkened. The yarn used for the webbing is dyed and rotproofed before being woven.

2. Characteristics.—There are three principal features in the new design of equipment :—

(a) A method of supporting the heavy contents of the large basic pouches to prevent down-drag of the equipment in front without counter-balance by weight on the back. To do this the braces form a sling : they are joined at the back where they cross and are fixed to the belt immediately at the rear of the basic pouches.

(b) An increase in the carrying capacity of the haversack and its additional fittings, and also an increase in size of the basic pouches.

(c) The equipment has been so designed that, if necessary, and when operating in tropical areas, the waistbelt can be worn loose without affecting the carriage of the equipment.

3. Fittings.—The ¾ inch, 1 inch and 2 inch 3-bar buckles and the 1 inch 4-bar buckle used have narrow spaces and the bar of each buckle to which the webbing is sewn is raised, to grip the straps securely and to prevent slipping through movement when the equipment is assembled.

The shoulder and haversack straps are fitted with a ¾ inch quick release buckle. This consists of two pieces: the upper with a centre bar and the lower without.

To fasten :—

(a) Pass the loose end of the strap up through both pieces, over the bar on the upper and down through both pieces.

(b) The strap goes from back to front of the pieces, that is, from the side where both pieces are joined to the strap to the side where they are open.

(c) To tighten the strap pull the loose end. If fastened correctly it will not slip.

(d) To release pull the short tab on the upper piece upwards and backwards.

The same buckle, 1 inch wide, is also fitted to the shoulder straps but without a tab as "quick-release" is not essential.

Instead of the former snap fasteners, a quick-release type is used on the basic pouches; this consists of a staple and link with a web tongue and tab for securing and release. Similar fasteners are provided to close the pockets on the sides of the haversack.

Components.

For Rank and File :—

Vocab. No.	Item.
(a) A.A. 2002	Belts, Waist, Normal (to fit 95 per cent. of troops).
A.A. 2001	Belts, Waist, Large.
(b) A.A. 2006	Frogs, Bayonet.
(c) A.A. 2011	Pouches, Basic, Left (with Bayonet Attachment).
(d) A.A. 2012	Pouches, Basic, Right.
(e) A.A. 2003	Braces (pairs).
(f) A.F. 0577	Covers, Bottles, Water, Aluminium.
(g) A.A. 2007	Haversacks (All Ranks).
(h) A.A. 2014	Straps, Shoulder, Haversack, Left.
A.A. 2015	,, ,, ,, Right.
(i) A.F. 0271	Rucksacks.

Additional Items :—

(j) A.F. 0101	Sheaths, Machete, 18 inch.
(k) A.F. 0236	Carriers, Tools, Entrenching '44 Pattern.
(l) A.A. 2000	Attachments, Brace (2 per set).—Personnel issued with items (m), (n), (o), (p), (r).
(m) A.A. 2005	Cases, Pistol—Personnel armed with Pistol.
(n) A.A. 2010	Pouches, ammunition, Pistol—Personnel armed with Pistol.
(o) A.A. 2004	Cases, Binocular ⎫ Personnel issued with
(p) A.A. 2009	Pockets, Compass ⎭ Binoculars and Compass.
(q) A.A. 2008	Haversacks (Officers)—Certain Officers only.
(r) A.A. 2013	Pouches, M.T. Driver—One each M.T. Driver in lieu of Basic Pouches, Left and Right.

A description of the above components is given in the following sub-paragraphs :—

Description.

(a) *Waistbelt.*—This is issued in two sizes, large and normal, having a maximum adjustment of 48 inches and 40 inches respectively. The normal size should fit 95 per cent. of troops. It is made in three parts (two side pieces and an adjustment strap) and the webbing is 2 inches wide. A closing buckle of the " hook and loop " type is fitted to the front ends of the side pieces and a double hook on each rear end ; a 1-inch link with gap is fitted diagonally to each side piece for attachment of the braces ; loops are provided for the spare ends of the adjustment strap. Two 1-inch 3-bar buckles are fitted to the back piece for attachment of the inner braces. Grommets (*i.e.*, eyelets with spur tooth washers) are fitted in the lower edge—four in each side piece and six centrally spaced in the adjustment strap; a 1 inch strap with snap fastener is fitted to the right-hand side piece to secure the rifle when slung on the shoulder.

(b) *Bayonet frog.*—This is provided with a woven hole in the upper scabbard loop to enable the No. 4, No. 5 or No. 7 bayonet to be carried by inserting the stud through the hole. The No. 1 bayonet is held in the frog in the usual way by the stud on the scabbard being inserted between the web loops. A narrow web loop is provided to slip over the hilt of the No. 1 or the No. 5 bayonet to prevent swinging.

(c) *Basic Pouch, Left.*—The internal dimensions are approximately $4\frac{1}{2}$ inches by 3 inches by $9\frac{1}{4}$ inches deep. On the back, two 2-inch wire hooks are provided for connecting to the waistbelt, a tapered chape with 1-inch 4-bar buckle for the braces and two vertical webbing loops for the haversack straps ; the hooded flap is fitted with the staple portion of a quick-release fastener which can be fitted to either of the two links on the front of the pouch. The normal method of closure is to use the bottom link ; the alternative method is for use when longer items are carried in the pouch. The left-hand side has loops as an alternative method of carrying the No. 4, 5 and 7 bayonet.

(d) *Basic Pouch, Right.*—Exactly the same as the left pouch except that bayonet loops are not fitted on the side.

(e) *Braces (pair).*—These have shoulder sections made of webbing 3 inches wide, with 1-inch wide front straps to connect to the basic pouches ; two 1-inch straps are sewn to the rear ends of the shoulder sections and stitched where they cross ; when fitted these are attached to the diagonals on the side pieces of the belt and are adjustable by the 3-bar buckles. The other two 1-inch straps which are not sewn where they cross are for attachment to the buckles on the back of the waistbelt.

(f) *Waterbottle Cover.*—This is a " bag " type to take the new aluminium waterbottle and cup. A pocket is provided inside on the back wall for the filter bag and has a small flap which prevents the bottle catching the top of the pocket; a web loop is fitted inside to take a tube of sterilizing tablets; the bottle is retained in the cover by flaps over its shoulders secured by snap fasteners. On the back a " hanger " hook is fitted for attachment to the grommets in the right side of the waistbelt.

(g) *Haversack*.—The dimensions of the haversack are approximately 8 inches by 6 inches by 10 inches deep, and it has a flap secured by two small straps and quick-release buckles. Side weather flaps are provided, and in each of these an eyelet is fitted to enable the flaps to be secured, if necessary, by a piece of string or cord. On each side is fitted a pocket approximately 6 inches by 2 inches by 8¼ inches deep, with a flap secured by a quick-release fastener; one pocket will accommodate the mess tin and the other rations or small kit. A 3-bar buckle is fitted to each side of the haversack, for attachment to the ends of the braces should it be necessary to carry it on the side. On the back, two 2-inch tabs are fitted for attachment to the shoulder straps; two loops are provided to tuck away spare ends of the shoulder straps. On the base are two 3-bar buckles for securing the ¾-inch diagonal straps forming part of the shoulder straps. For carrying the bedding two long ¾-inch straps with quick release buckles are fitted to the base. Sleeves are provided to enable these straps to be stowed away when not in use.

There are the following attachments; a chape with two grommets and a horizontal strap (a portion of which is reinforced) with a quick release buckle. These are both attached to the flap. A small buckle chape and tab are fixed to the bottom edge.

These can be used for carriage of tools. When carrying the shovel the strap with the quick release buckle should be wound twice round the shaft, and when carrying a pick the strap (reinforced portion) will be passed first round the head of the pick then round the shaft. At each bottom back corner of the haversack a strap is sewn, one having a 3-bar buckle and the other a tip; these pass through one or both of the web loops on the back of the basic pouches and connect round the body in front. This is particularly useful when crawling to prevent sag of heavily laden pouches, or to retain the haversack in position when quick action is anticipated.

NOTE.—The back and base of the haversack is lined with waterproof cloth to prevent penetration of moisture from the body.

(h) *Shoulder Straps*.—These are made left and right; each consists of an integrally woven shoulder section, 2 inches wide tapering to 1 inch, to carry a quick-release buckle through which a strap with a hook is adjustable. To the " ear " on the side of the hook is sewn a narrow side supporting (or diagonal) strap which is adjustable through a quick-release buckle on a short strap, having a tip on the end for attachment to the corresponding buckle on the base of the haversack.

(i) *Rucksack*.—This is made of light weight duck; its dimensions are approximately 14 inches by 6 inches by 18 inches deep (fully open). Large eyelets are equally spaced in the top hem and a draw cord is provided. It has a large closing flap having a flat pocket on the underside 8 inches deep, fitted with two partitions and a flap secured by quick-release fasteners. The large flap is closed by two ¾-inch web straps and quick-release buckles. A large pocket about 10 inches by 3 inches by 12 inches deep, is provided on the front of the rucksack and there are pockets on each side, 6 inches by 3 inches by 12 inches deep. All three pockets have "hooded" flaps with quick-release fasteners. The inner faces of the main closing flap and the centre pocket, as well as the inside of the hooded flap of this pocket, are lined with light-weight waterproof material. Webbing tabs and loops are fitted to the back and buckles on the base for attachment of the shoulder straps previously described. Straps for an entrenching tool, similar to those on the haversack, are provided. On each side of the back wall of the rucksack three 1-inch "D" rings are fitted, equally spaced, to enable the rucksack to be secured to the Manpack Carrier, G.S., when required.

Additional Items :—

(j) *Machete Sheath*.—This is made entirely of selvedged webbings and is constructed to give adequate reinforcement. A "channel" is formed inside down one side to enable the machete to be easily inserted. A sheradized brass mouthpiece is fitted and on the back is a "hanger" hook for the attachment to the grommets in the waist-belt or, when desired, to the flap of the haversack.

(k) *Entrenching Tool Carrier*.—A simple cover with a quick release buckle is attached to the equipment by means of a "hanger" hook.

(l) *Brace Attachments*.—These are interchangeable. Each consists of 1-inch webbing doubled and sewn to give rigidity, two 2-inch wire double hooks for attachment to the waistbelt and a 4-bar buckle for the brace at the top, below which is a link to receive the free end of the brace.

(m) *Pistol Case*.—This is made to accommodate the present Service revolver. The body is woven in one piece and is lined with smooth webbing; the flap is closed with a quick-release fastener. Two double hooks are provided on the back for attachment to the waist-belt as well as a "hanger" hook to attach to the ammunition pouch when that article is to be carried above the pistol case, or to serve as an alternative method of attachment to the waistbelt.

(n) *Ammunition Pouch*.—This is a woven article for pistol ammunition. It is provided with a "box-like" lid secured by a quick-release fastener. In the flange at the bottom two grommets are fitted for attachment to the pistol case and on the back two vertical web loops for carrying on the belt in an alternative position; a horizontal loop is fitted to pass over the brace attachment.

(o) *Binocular Case.*—This is made of a double "shell" of webbing interlined with felt, a fibre stiffening is fitted in the base. The hooded lid is provided with a quick-release fastener. On the back two double hooks and a "hanger" hook are fitted, similar to those on the pistol case.

(p) *Compass Pocket.*—Similar in all respects to the ammunition pouch except that it is lined with felt and has a fibre stiffening to protect the compass.

(q) *Officers' Haversack.*—This is a rectangular bag of dimensions (approximately) 13 inches by 2 inches by 9 inches deep, with a flap secured by one strap and buckle. The interior is lined with light waterproof material. Two buckles are provided on the back for attachment to the brace ends and a loop at the top to enable the haversack to be carried by hand, when desired.

(r) *Basic Pouch, M.T. Drivers.*—This is similar in size and construction to the left basic pouch, except that, in place of the attachments on the back, a 2-inch wide web loop is provided to enable it to be carried on the waistbelt to the rear of the brace attachment.

To Assemble the Equipment.

As has been previously stated, the design of the equipment permits a variety of combinations of the several articles to suit all arms, and the following instructions will be carefully observed :—

4. Set for Rank and File.—Fit the waistbelt (a) reasonably loose. Adjustment is made by withdrawing the double hooks (on the rear ends of the side pieces) from the loops woven inside the adjustment strap and re-inserting them a corresponding distance from each end of the adjustment strap. Once the belt is fitted it need only be altered when worn separately with side arms.

Slip the bayonet frog (b) over the left end of the belt, so that it hangs near the double hook.

Attach the basic pouches left and right (c) and (d) on the outside of the belt by passing the double hooks over the upper and lower edges of the belt and inserting the hooks into the loops woven inside the side-pieces of the belt, so that they correspond each side, bringing the buckles on top of the pouches in line with the centre of the shoulders.

Lay the braces (e) out flat with the buckles uppermost. Pass the left and right front ends through the centre opening of the buckle on top of the respective basic pouches and secure them in position about 5 inches from the taper of the braces. Insert the back loop ends in the links on the sides of the belt and adjust them to the length required to fit snugly to the body so that each basic pouch is supported by a sling. This new method of suspension can best be demonstrated at this stage by filling the basic pouches and testing the balance and adjusting as necessary. It will be noted that the two brace ends as yet unattached to the centre back portion of the belt are not brought into use and the load can be effectively carried without fastening the belt. Attach the two loose rear ends of the braces to the buckles on the back of the belt and adjust them, taking care that they do not relieve the rear side ends of any tension. These two straps are only required to support the weight of any article which may be attached to the rear centre portion of the belt. Finally pass the free front ends of the braces down behind the pouch, between the web chape carrying the buckle and the back of the pouch.

Care should be taken that the counter-balancing straps (attached to the sides of the belt) are adjusted to fit snugly round the body so that each basic pouch and its contents is supported, in effect by two complete slings to prevent down-drag of the equipment in front. This adjustment can be tested by putting the equipment on and leaving the waistbelt unfastened. Since there is no need to help to support the weight by tightening the waistbelt, there will be more comfort and ventilation.

Attach the waterbottle cover (*f*) by means of the "hanger" hook on the back to the rear pair of grommets fitted in the right-hand side piece of the waistbelt. (This is the normal position, but the hanger hooks can be attached to the grommets in any position desired).

The foundation of the equipment is thus formed, and is now put on ready for attachment of the haversack (*g*) which is previously fitted to suit the wearer as follows :—

For men of average height the movable buckles on the shoulder straps (*h*) should be placed approximately 5 inches from the end of each strap. Attach the tabs on the back of the haversack to these buckles close to the point of attachment and insert the spare ends of the straps under the web loops. With the front tabs carrying, the hooks equally adjusted, sling the haversack on the shoulders and secure the hooks to the top bars of the buckles on the basic pouches. Now ascertain whether the front tabs are correctly adjusted to bring the tapered portion of the shoulder straps in line with the tapers of the braces, and secondly, note whether the top of the haversack is approximately in line with the shoulders. Make any necessary correction in the position of the movable buckles and re-attach the haversack tabs. Taking care not to twist the side supporting (diagonal) straps, attach them to the respective buckles on the base of the haversack. The haversack is now ready to be put on with the side supporting straps slack. Attach the hooks to the buckles at the top of the basic pouches, and pull the free ends of the side supporting straps forward in an upward direction just sufficiently tight to balance the weight of the filled haversack.

To prevent movement of the haversack on the back as well as to keep the top of the basic pouches close to the body, the retaining straps at the bottom corners of the haversack (left with 3-bar buckle and right with tip) are passed through the forward loops on the back of the basic pouches and fastened comfortably tight in front.

If the foregoing instructions are carefully carried out, the equipment will be found comfortable, with the load well balanced and evenly distributed.

5. Rucksack (i).—To carry the rucksack on the back with the equipment, it is necessary to detach the shoulder straps (h) from the haversack and transfer these to the rucksack, normally leaving the movable buckles in the same position as when used with the haversack, and taking care to adjust the side supporting straps sufficiently taut to support the weight carried.

The haversack may then be carried at the left side by attaching the free ends of the braces to the buckles on the sides of the haversack.

NOTE.—The retaining straps sewn to the bottom corners of the haversack should be fastened fairly tightly back over the front of the haversack to keep them in position and the free end of the long strap neatly tied to the other strap.

6. Machete Sheath (j).—With the bayonet frog moved to the rear, the sheath may be attached, by means of the "hanger" hook, to a pair of grommets in the left side piece of the waistbelt; or, if preferred, the sheath may be attached to the tab with grommets on the flap of the haversack and held by the central strap at the bottom (front) of the haversack, should these not be used for any other purpose. Like the waterbottle cover it can also be fitted to any grommets on the belt as an alternative.

Weights of Component Parts.

	lb.	oz.
Waistbelt (Normal)		6¾
Bayonet, Frog ..		1¼
Basic Pouch, Left..		10¾
,, ,, Right		10½
Braces		6¼
Waterbottle Cover		5¾
Haversack ..	1	7¼
Shoulder Straps (pair)		5¼

4 lb. 6¼ oz.

Other Items.	lb.	oz.
Rucksack (less Shoulder Straps)	2	5
Machete Sheath		6¾
Entrenching Tool Carrier (proposed)		
Brace attachments (2)		3¼
Pistol Case		6¼
Ammunition Pouch		2
Binocular Case		10
Compass Pocket		2¾
Officers' Haversack		10½

Additional Items for Officers, Warrant Officers, N.C.Os. and Specialists.

7. Brace attachments are issued for the use of those not equipped with basic pouches or with only one basic pouch.

The following articles are attached in a variety of ways :—

Pistol Case ;
Ammunition Pouch ;
Binocular Case ;
Compass Pocket.

For example, the pistol case with the ammunition pouch above may be worn on the left side of the belt (over the brass attachment) and in a similar manner the binocular case with the compass pocket above on the right side ; or the ammunition pouch on the right side of the belt with the pistol case to the rear, may be hooked in the grommets in the side-piece of the belt, and the compass pocket above the binocular case on the left side of the belt. With this combination the waterbottle would be carried on the left side. Alternatively, it will be seen that to meet any desired variations a basic pouch may be used on one side and either a binocular case or pistol case with the respective pouch on the other.

To Assemble.

8. Fit the waistbelt (*a*) as before described.

Attach the brace attachments (*l*) to the side pieces of the belt in line with the shoulders, by passing the two double hooks over the edges of the belt and inserting them into the loops woven inside.

Attach the rear ends of the braces (*e*) and the counter-balancing straps to the belt as previously described and pass the left and right front ends of the braces through the centre opening of the buckle at the top of each brace attachment, to within about 5 inches from the taper of the brace and secure ; then pass the free end through the link below the buckle.

The assembly should now be tried on, and any necessary adjustments made to the six points of connection of the braces. Note the position of the brace attachment buckles by marking a pencil line across the braces against the buckles.

Connect the pistol case (*m*) to the ammunition pouch (*n*) by the " hanger " hook. Unfasten the front end of the left brace, pass the brace attachment buckle through the horizontal web loop on the back of the ammunition pouch, and connect the pistol case to the belt by the double hooks, which are inserted in the woven loops each side of the brace attachment hooks ; then re-connect the front end of the brace to the brace attachment as described above.

The binocular case (*o*) and the compass pocket (*p*) are attached in the same way over the brace attachment on the right side.

The waterbottle cover (*f*) is attached by inserting the "hanger" hook to the grommets in the right side-piece of belt.

9. *As an alternative* the binocular case with the compass pocket above it can be worn on the left side. The ammunition pouch can then be attached to the belt on the right side by first detaching the brace attachment from the belt, passing the belt through one loop on the back of the pouch, re-fixing the brace attachment to the belt and finally passing the belt through the other loop on the pouch, so that the pouch straddles the brace attachment. The pistol case is then attached by the " hanger " hook to one pair of grommets in the right side-piece of the belt. With this combination the waterbottle cover is transferred to the left side of the belt.

The equipment is now ready to put on. The haversack (*g*) with shoulder straps (*h*) fitted as previously described, is put on separately and connected to the brace attachment buckles by the shoulder strap hooks ; the retaining straps at the bottom corners of the haversack are fastened round the body tightly enough to be comfortable.

The officers' haversack (*q*) may be carried on one side of the equipment by attaching the ends of the braces to the buckles on the back of the haversack.

10. The set of equipment for those armed with a pistol only is assembled and adjusted as previously described, the pistol case being attached to the left side and the ammunition pouch to the right side of the belt, or, if preferred, the pistol case can be connected to the ammunition pouch by the " hanger " hook to hang below the belt on the right side.

11. The set for non-combatant units is similarly assembled, without the pistol case and ammunition pouch.

12. The set for M.T. drivers is likewise assembled, with the basic pouch (*r*) carried on the waistbelt in rear of the brace attachment on either side, in accordance with the type of vehicle being driven.

Care and Preservation of the Equipment.

13. Scrubbing, bleaching and the use of Blanco on the equipment is forbidden.

An Army Council Instruction will be published on the types of renovator which will be used to restore colour or water repellency. No other types will be used than those approved.

PLATES.

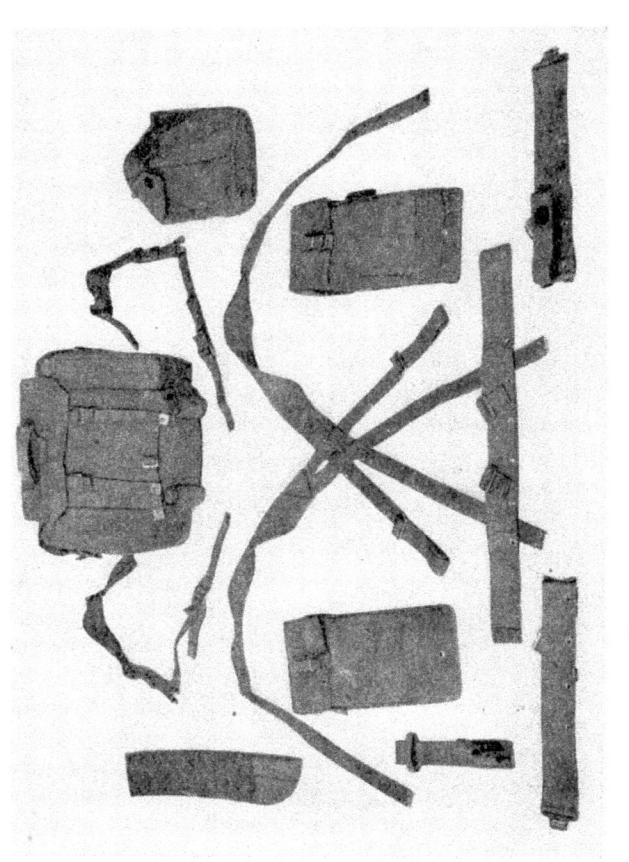

PLATE I.—The equipment unassembled.

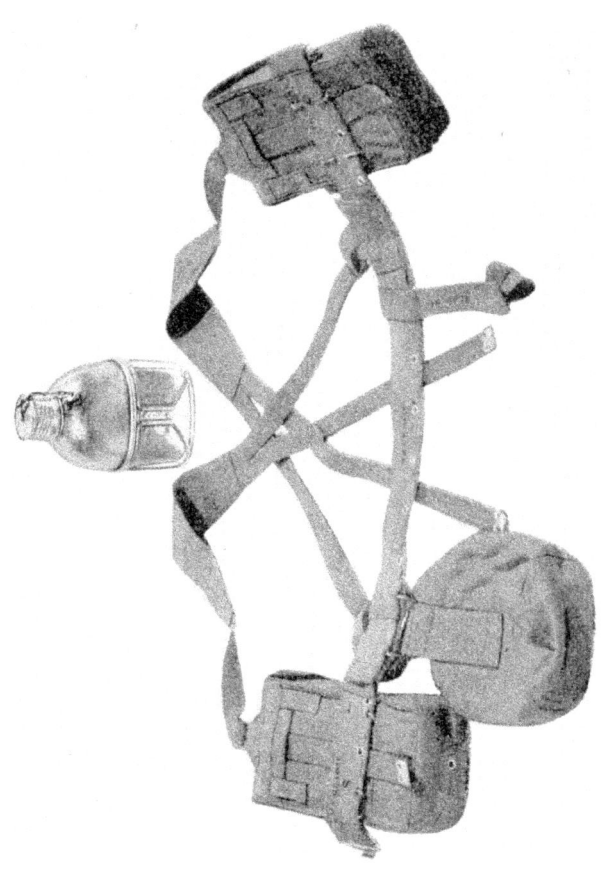

PLATE II.—Equipment assembled, showing inside view and waterbottle.

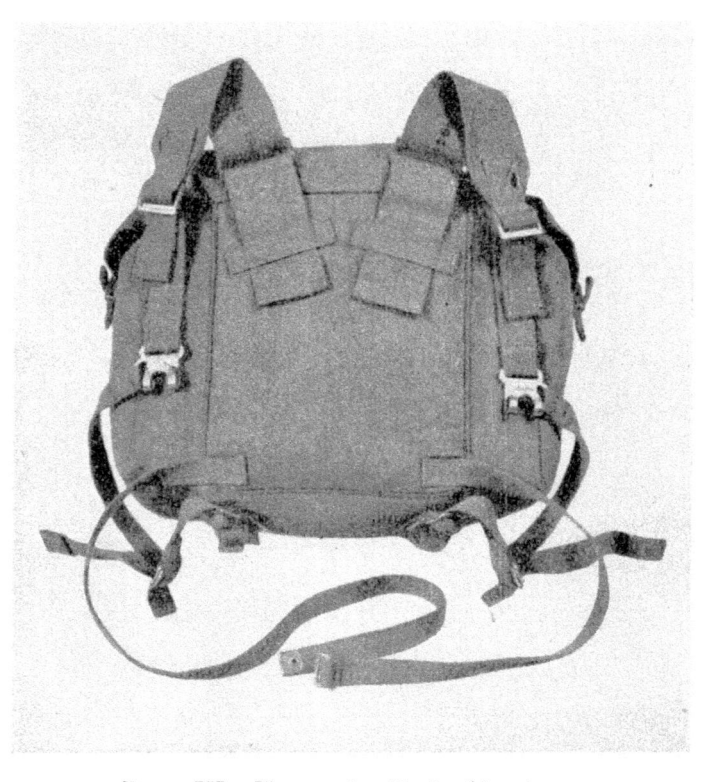

PLATE III.—Haversack with shoulder straps.

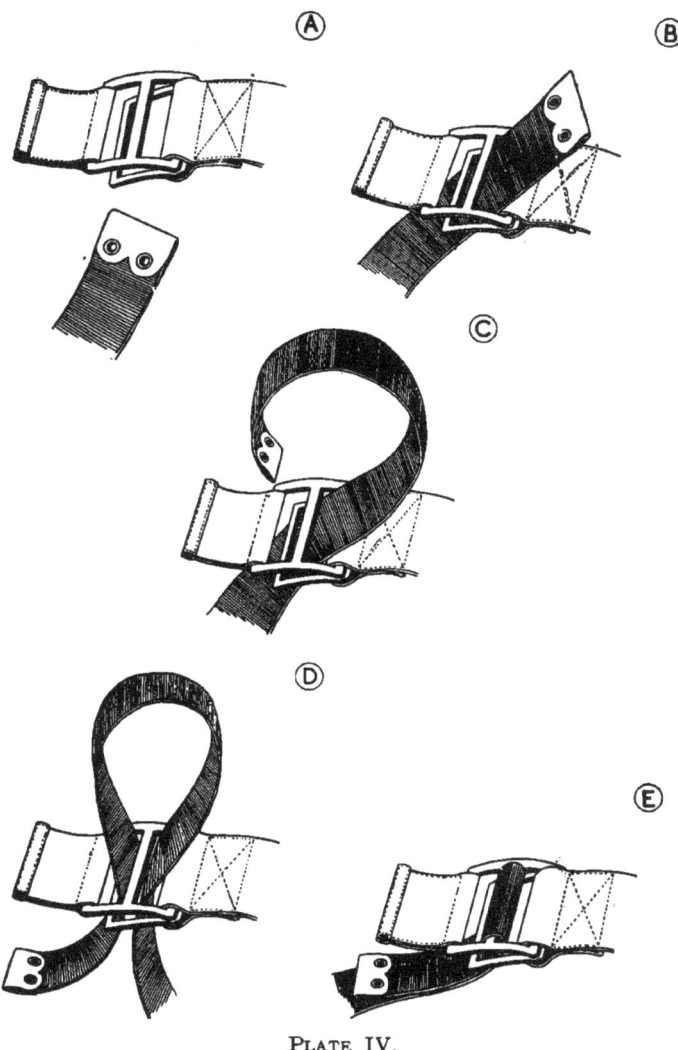

PLATE IV.

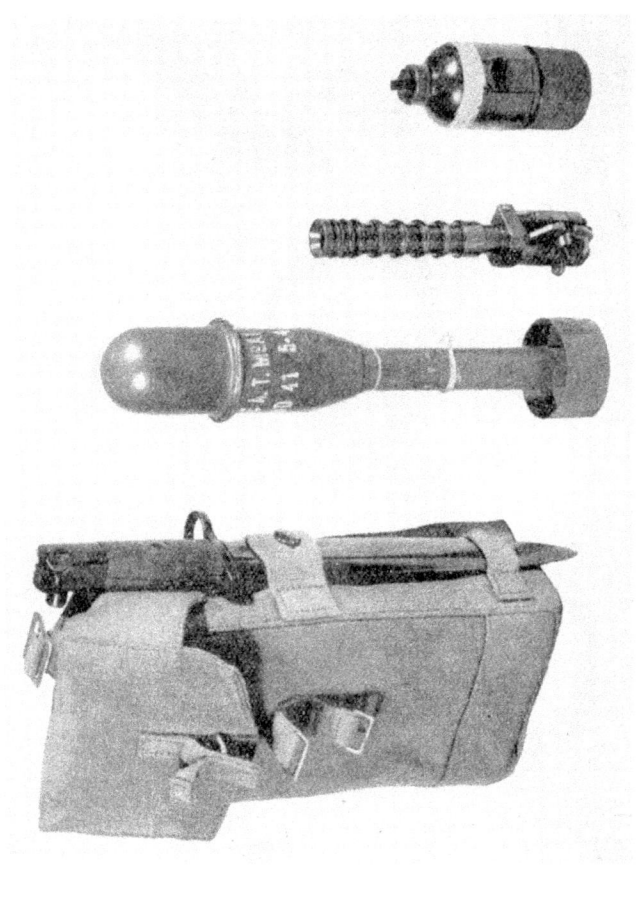

PLATE V.—Left basic pouch showing double quick-release fastening and alternative method of carrying bayonet.

PLATE VI.—Front view.

(SÒ 1447) B 3

PLATE VII.—Rear view without haversack.

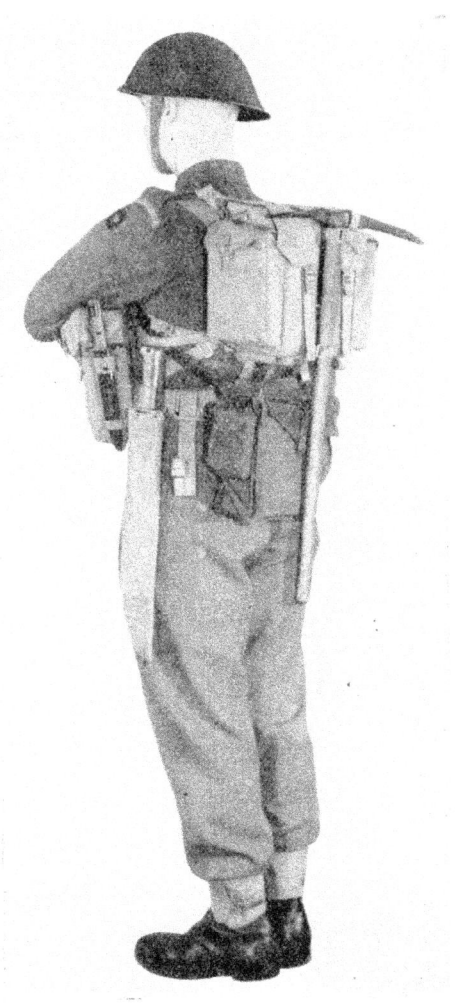

PLATE VIII.—Left side showing bayonet on basic pouch, machete in sheath and lightened pick attached to haversack.

PLATE IX.—Right side showing rifle slung and position of waterbottle.

PLATE X.—Rear view showing method of carriage of the bedding roll under the haversack, and lightened shovel.

PLATE XI.—Rear view showing the bedding role strapped round the haversack, also lightened shovel with a web cover.

PLATE XII.—Showing clearance between helmet and shovel blade when in the prone position.

PLATE XIII.—Rucksack with closing flap raised to show kit-bag type fastening of the main compartment.

PLATE XIV.—Rucksack carried with the equipment.

PLATE XV.—Man-pack Carrier G.S. worn over the equipment.

PLATE XVI.—Rucksack attached to the manpack Carrier G.S. worn over the equipment.

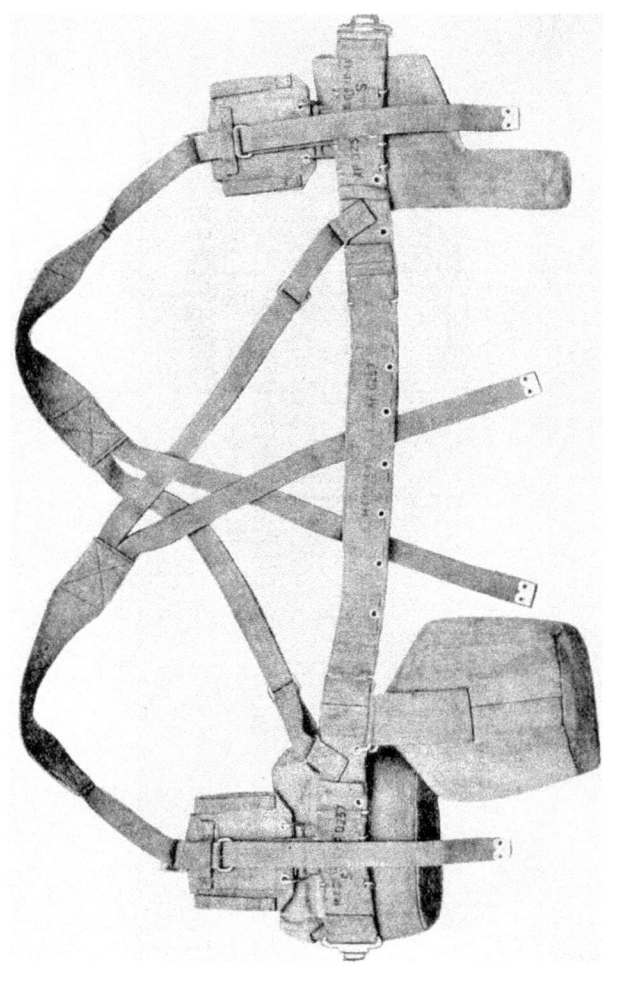

PLATE XVII.—Equipment assembled for officers.

PLATE XVIII.—Front view of the equipment for officers, certain warrant officers, N.C.Os. and specialists.

PLATE XIX.—Alternative position of articles in front.

PLATE XX.—Equipment for those armed with a pistol only.

PLATE XXI.—Equipment for non-combatant units.

PLATE XXII.—Showing the basic pouch for M.T. drivers.

www.ingramcontent.com/pod-product-compliance
Lightning Source LLC
Chambersburg PA
CBHW040312050426
42450CB00020B/3468